CASTE,

IN THE

ISLAND OF CEYLON.

BOSTON:
PRESS OF T. R. MARVIN, 42 CONGRESS STREET.
1853.

Note.—This letter, addressed to Dr. Anderson, one of the Secretaries of the American Board of Commissioners for Foreign Missions, is intended to furnish a convenient answer to inquiries from those friends of missions, who desire to know the views and proceedings of the Ceylon Mission in relation to Caste. It professes to be applicable, as it really is, only to the somewhat peculiar District occupied by that mission on the Island of Ceylon. Our knowledge of Caste on the Continent, and of the methods of treating it resorted to by the different missions there, must be gained from the competent witnesses that are residing on the spot.

Missionary House, August 25, 1853.

CASTE, IN CEYLON.

Jaffna, Ceylon, August 6, 1852.

Dear Sir,—We will now attempt an answer to the inquiries contained in your letter of Dec. 16, 1851, on the subject of Caste. And we must commence by saying, that it is a very intricate and difficult subject. We do not mean to say, that it is difficult to define caste, as set forth in the Shastras of the Hindoos, or as it originally existed, and perhaps still exists, on the Continent of India. But caste, as it exists in this Province, has been greatly modified by many causes, which have been long in operation. For three centuries and a half, the people have been under the dominion of the Portuguese, the Dutch, and the English. All these governments did much, if not to exterminate, at least greatly to modify caste. Many of the people have, for a long period, been familiar with many of the truths and forms of Christianity. And though caste still has an existence among us, it has been so modified, by these and other causes, that some of its original features are now scarcely visible.

In answering the question, *What is Caste?* (as it exists on the Continent of India,) we cannot do better than to give you the following extract from a document published by the Madras Missionary Conference, in 1850. It is as follows:

"Caste, which is a distinction among the Hindoos, founded upon supposed birth-purity and impurity, is in its nature essentially a religious institution, and not a mere civil distinction. The Institutes of Menu and other Shastras regard the division of the people into four castes, as of divine appointment. We find, also, that stringent laws were enacted for upholding this important part of the Hindoo religion. Future rewards are decreed to those who retain it, and future punishments to those who violate it. The Hindoos of the present day believe, that the preservation or loss of caste deeply affects their future destiny. In the Madras Memorial to the Supreme Government, dated April 2, 1845, they declare that the loss of caste is connected with the vitality of the Hindoo religion.

"On the scale of caste, wealth, talents, industry, and moral character, confer no elevation; and the absence of these imposes no degradation. It is ceremonial pollution alone, which destroys it. This may be conveyed to a person of high caste through the sight, the taste, or the touch of one of an inferior grade. Such an institution, therefore, can never be called a mere civil distinction; for whatever it may have been in its origin, it is now adopted as an essential part of the Hindoo religion."

This is undoubtedly a correct definition of caste, where it exists in its purity. But, by a concise history of its developments, as it has come before us in this Province, you will readily perceive how greatly it has been modified by the causes above mentioned, and in how few particulars caste, as it exists here, is correctly delineated by the definition quoted above.

The strict notion of birth-purity, or impurity, in a religious sense, as defined in the above extract, is not, so far as we can ascertain, very generally believed in this province. The brahmins, and probably some others, believe it; and there are, probably, some indefinite notions on this point still lingering in the minds of many. But the brahmins in this province are comparatively few; and as a body, they have ever stood aloof from Christian instructions, and claim a maintenance from the people on the ground of their being incarnate divinities. Their claims however, on this ground, are admitted by the people only to a limited extent, as their whole demeanor towards them sufficiently shows. Brahmins on the Continent make light of the pretensions of brahmins in Ceylon, because, as they affirm, their continental ancestors by crossing the sea, and taking food under such circumstances, lost their caste-purity. On the other hand the Ceylon brahmins very justly affirm, on the authority of the Shastras, that the continental brahmins have undeniably vitiated their caste by serving as magistrates, interpreters, writers, and in various other secular employments, for a livelihood; and that, too, in the service of foreigners of an unclean race, the Europeans. In our remarks, therefore, upon this subject, we may well leave the brahmins, on both sides of the water, out of the question; both because they have pronounced sentence upon each other; and because we, in Ceylon, have no brahmins in our mission communities, either in our churches, or in our service, as school-masters or native assistants.

But though little is said in this Province of "birth-purity or impurity," which on the Continent is considered so essential to the Hindoo doctrine of caste, yet on other grounds much is said of pure or impure caste, or classes of society. In this, regard is had, not merely to their birth, but to their diet and regimen, corresponding customs and manners,—their social avocations, intellectual habits, and religious employments. Between the two extremes of the pure Sivan, on the one hand, who rigidly confines himself to a simple vegetable diet—consequently abstaining from everything that has had animal life—down to the Pariah, on the other hand, who is unscrupulous about his food, sometimes eating even carrion, and using intoxicating drinks, with corresponding habits and customs; the Hindoo population is divided into numerous classes, irrespective of caste distinctions. Sivans, for instance, who are vegetarians, are generally of the Vellala caste. But all Vellalas are not Sivans, nor are all Sivans Vellalas. Those who eat only shrimps, account themselves superior to those who eat fish; and those who eat only shrimps and fish, superior to those who eat eggs and fowls. Thus on, indefinitely, downward to the Pariah. Thus, without any very prevalent belief in "birth-purity or impurity" in this Province, there are substantial grounds for the distinctions of pure and impure classes. And they also maintain their claims to purity of caste on the ground of their customs, secular avocations, intellectual habits and religious employments, as mentioned above. One obvious reason for the absence of the strict Hindoo notion of caste, in this Province, arises from the fact, that the doctrine of the Bible, regarding the origin of the human race, is here very extensively known. This arises from the fact before mentioned, that the people have for so long a period been under the control of powerful Christian governments. The Dutch, especially, used systematic measures, on a large scale, to instruct the youth, and to convert the Hindoos to the Christian faith. In the early part of the eighteenth century, nearly the whole of the rising generation of males were embodied in schools, established and sustained by the Dutch government. In the Elemen tary Catechism universally used in these schools, the history of Adam and Eve, and of their immediate descendants, is given. Even to this day we occasionally meet with a man of great age, who will repeat to us the old Dutch Catechism, a great part of which we early incorporated into the Elementary Catechism now in use in our schools. But this Scripture doctrine, so far as it is admitted, is wholly subversive of the Hindoo doctrine of caste. We have never known any individual who belonged to our church, who did not profess fully to believe the Scripture doctrine on this subject.

What, then, is caste *in Jaffna?* This is a point, on which we are anxious that the Committee be accurately and fully informed.

As a general definition, we may say, that caste in Jaffna is a perpetuation of caste and caste-institutions from the Continent, modified by a combination of causes incidental to foreign immigration and colonization; under the rule, in the first instance, of revolutionizing and conquering native princes; and subsequently, for a long period, under the reign of three of the most powerful governments of Europe, each of which, in its own peculiar way and manner, did much for the transformation of the native inhabitants. Hence it is not strange, that caste should be so greatly modified in this Province. But let us not be misunderstood. It still exists, even here, and shows its sharp and ugly horns and cloven feet in the midst of us. We wish we were not compelled to add, that we see and feel its baneful influence in some of the members of our churches. It is, indeed, a prominent and troublesome feature of Hindoo society, ever presenting obstacles of various kinds to the progress of Christianity. The nature and tendency of the institution is unsocial, forbidding, and aristocratic; pervading all castes and classes of society, and quite as manifest in the low caste, as in the high; each caste, as they suppose, having some peculiar grounds for boasting.

That we may further elucidate the subject, it is necessary that we proceed to give some of the results of our own experience and observations on the subject; and then show by what means Hindoo caste has been so greatly modified in Jaffna; and also, to what transforming influences it is still subjected.

Before coming to this country, we had formed our ideas of caste in India mainly by what we had read in the journals of early missionaries in Bengal—Carey, Marshman, Ward, and others; and of course our minds were much awake to the importance of "breaking caste" in the mission field, especially as we were led to understand that it might be broken by so trifling a circumstance as that of partaking of a meal in a missionary's house. One of our first encounters with caste, which happened a few days after our arrival in 1816, was a trifling incident in connection with a horse-keeper. On his being directed to do something in adjusting the furniture about the house, he refused to obey, saying it was contrary to his caste to do the work. But as we could not tolerate caste on our premises, we told him he must obey or quit our service. To the latter he very readily assented, leaving the missionary to take care of his own horse, as there was no other horse-keeper in the parish. This was the first of a series of events, by which we became gradually acquainted with the state of persons and things in the country, in relation to caste. By this we were taught, that it was quite impracticable, without sails, oars or steam, to propel *our* frail bark against the prevailing monsoon! And surely there can be no marvel that it should thus happen to the much frailer bark of timid, recently converted Hindoos.

After a few weeks' residence, we commenced a day

school on our premises, taught by a young man who was formerly a pupil in Mr. Palm's school. This man was able to bring to the school a few children belonging to his own family circle; but the neighbors generally considered it polluting and vitiating to caste for their children to come and learn on our premises. As soon, however, as the practice, by slow degrees, became common in the parish, all fears on the subject of caste vanished.

From and after the year 1818, we passed through a similar process in the admission of boys to our boarding schools. This very novel procedure produced a deeper sensation of alarm in the public mind, than that produced by bringing children into our day school; consequently our progress was much slower, and more difficult. Eating and drinking on the premises of Christians, was thought to be utterly destructive to the children's caste, and a disgrace to their parents. In process of time, however, after many were committed to the practice who *could* keep each other in countenance, and when it was seen that their children were not changed into Englishmen, or Portuguese, but were much improved in body and mind, their fears on the subject of caste gradually subsided, leaving us to prosecute this branch of missionary labor to as great an extent as we thought proper.

A still deeper tone of alarm was sounded, when we began to receive girls into our boarding schools. But this, also, gradually died away, as harmless as in the case of boys, leaving us to prosecute our plans at pleasure.

From the ideas we then entertained on the subject of "breaking caste," and even from what we had recently learned from the talk of the people, we thought it most incongruous that any in either of our boarding schools should ever boast themselves of caste. We had "broken" and "killed" it. But in process of time we were called to "break" it and "kill" it again. And we resolutely did it. In the "Central boarding school" at Tillipally, then under the care of Mr. Woodward, in the year 1824 or 1825, it was ascertained that there were low-caste boys in the school. This was an offence to certain of the Vellalas, who made an attempt to have low-caste boys removed; declaring, that though they might with impunity eat with persons of their own caste on mission premises, they could not and would not eat with those of an inferior caste. This controversy led, ultimately, to the expulsion of three or four of the oldest and most influential high-caste boys in the school. They soon, however, saw reason to repent of their conduct, and humbly sought and obtained admission to the school.

In 1821, when it became known that the two first converts from Hindooism, members of our boarding school, were about to be received into the church, so strong was the opposition to such a procedure, that we had reason to expect violent attempts would be made to rescue one of the candidates. The occasion, however, passed off without disturbance, and was one of great interest in the history of the mission. It was indeed a strange sight to the spectators, to see two of their countrymen, of the Vellala caste, not only publicly eating and drinking with foreigners, but partaking with them from the same cup and plate. This was something in advance of all that had been previously witnessed as an outrage upon caste-principle; and was quite sufficient, we should suppose, to stamp the young novitiates as outcasts from Hindooism. Some apology was, however, made for them by their heathen relatives, that the boys were young, and knew not what they were doing. But a farther advance was soon made, and another severe blow inflicted upon caste, when, at the close of the same year, two adult converts from heathenism, who were men of different castes, were admitted to the church, and sat down together at the table of the Lord. Subsequently another, and yet another fatal blow was inflicted, when females, first from our boarding school, and then adult women were publicly admitted to the church by baptism, and thus led to commune with persons of different castes and occupations. At our great meeting in 1825, when we admitted candidates from our several stations, at a large central bungalow in Santillipy, prepared for the purpose, there were still more decided and daring manifestations of opposition on the part of relatives. The elder brother of one of the candidates stood up in the meeting, and boisterously protested against his brother being received into the church. But the presence of a police officer prevented open violence. In January, 1821, when the first professed convert from Hindooism was about to be received into the church at Batticotta, so strong was the opposition of his relatives that they carried him off by force the day before he was to have been received, and kept him in close confinement for some time. We might easily multiply examples of this kind, but the above are sufficient.

As substitutes for further specifications, we may observe generally, that for thirty years past hundreds of pupils of both sexes, and of different castes, have been boarded and educated in our two seminaries, at Batticotta and Oodooville; that, of the pupils thus instructed, about one hundred and twenty couples have been married—generally at Oodooville; that after the solemnization of the marriage in the church, and the partaking of a little fruit at the station, the bride and bridegroom repair, with their friends, to the house of their parents, who are mostly heathen, where a marriage feast is prepared for the friends and relatives of both parties, whether heathen or Christian, and without attempting to compel Christians to conform to the heathen ceremonies. Sometimes it happens, that the newly married couple take up their abode permanently at the house of one of their parents, sharing the homestead, it may be, with two or three other families who are entirely heathen. It should be remarked here, however, that native Christians, when thus situated, are careful not to give unnecessary offence to their heathen relatives. In a very few cases our female pupils, who were members of the church, have married heathen husbands; and in many cases graduates from the seminary at Batticotta, whether church members or not, have married heathen wives. But we now hear little or nothing of caste being vitiated by these marriage alliances; and this too, whether one or both of the parties after marriage live as Christians or otherwise.

When this state of things was related to our missionary brethren at Calcutta, they exclaimed with surprise, mingled with some degree of unbelief, "And will they talk of caste after that?" But the climax is yet to be stated. Franciscus Malayapa, a native assistant employed by the mission, and subsequently licensed by us as a native preacher, had adopted the European dress, before he came into our service. For a time, and for convenience sake, he boarded at the table of one of the mission families. His father-in-law, the Rev. Christain David, (recently deceased at the age of eighty-one,) was, for the space of forty years from the time of his adopting the European dress, in the habit of eating, whenever occasion offered, at the tables of the principal Europeans in the Island, beginning at the Governor's table in the days of General and Lady Brownrigg. But neither the father-in-law, nor the son-in-law supposed, for a moment, that they had lost or injured their caste. But on the contrary, thought much of their caste, and that they had bettered their condition by intercourse with Europeans. Nor did the community at large cast them off because of their dress, or because of their connection with foreigners; though when provoked to do it they might mention these facts as a blot. And thus it is now with many, who had been educated at Batticotta, and who hold important offices in the country, some of whom adopted European customs. Under this aspect of the subject, we see that caste is indicative of one's ancestry, and that it is not a common and easy thing for a man, in this Province, to " break or lose caste."

We close this topic by giving prominence to the fact, that notwithstanding the manifold aggressions we have made upon caste through the period of more than thirty years, there has been no case of native converts, whether young or old, male or female, being wholly and finally cut off from the family circle, or unable to abide in the place wherein they were called, in consequence of their having broken caste by becoming Christians. We do not say that this would not have been the case, had the conduct of our native Christians been more offensive. In most cases they are very careful not to give offence to their heathen relatives—in some cases too much so. Weak as they are, it would not be strange if they frequently conform too much to the wishes of friends and relatives, who are still heathens.

We have indeed seen cases, in which heathen wives have left their husbands for a little season; in which parents have shown great displeasure, and even banished their children from the house, for a time, because they were baptized and received into the Christian church; and very great annoyances have been experienced by native converts, especially in regard to the observance of the Sabbath, while living among their heathen relatives; and these difficulties were greater in former times than at present. But the fact of native converts, whether married or unmarried, being tolerated in the house and family of their heathen relatives, shows most clearly that caste, in the sense of the Shastras, has been greatly modified in this Province; and that "losing caste," is not here an easy or common thing.

We will now speak of what the Hindoos themselves have done, and are still doing, for the destruction of caste in this Province.

1. The continental Pandian kings, who formerly reigned in Jaffna, introduced a new caste into the Province, called Madapalies—the offspring of high-caste men with Covia women, who are a high caste of domestic slaves. This caste was endowed with certain perquisites and privileges, so that it now ranks among the high castes of the country, next below the Vellala. This caste cannot boast much of "birth purity," though they are not regarded as an impure caste. The caste of Madapalies, into which it is comparatively easy to get introduced, is not found among the ninety-six castes of Southern India, and is peculiar to this Province. But the introduction of a new caste, and one of so great importance, must manifestly vitiate the whole system of Hindoo caste, as taught in the Shastras.

2. The Hindoos in this Province are destroying the remains of this evil system, by constantly rising from a lower to a higher caste. Such a process must of itself be as gross a violation of the classic Hindoo system of caste, as can well be conceived of. Methods of rising from one caste to another are various.

(1.) By false entries, when persons remove from one place to another where their ancestors are not known.

(2.) By bribing those who have charge of the registries in public offices, to insert their names in higher castes.

(3.) This is done extensively by intermarriages.

This third method is deserving of some special illustration, as bearing extensively on the subject in hand, in relation to the higher castes. For example: two young men of the Vellala caste, graduates of the seminary at Batticotta, accepted large pecuniary offers from a man of wealth, but of lower caste, at Colombo, to marry his two daughters—both heathens and uneducated. The young men immediately proceeded to Colombo, and took possession of their prizes. Hitherto they have lived in good style and in credit, having employments suited to their education. Moreover, they are sustained by the public opinion of their countrymen, inasmuch as they have obtained a fair *quid pro quo.* The father-in-law made a good speculation, because his grand-children will be registered according to the rank of their father, as Vellalas. True, they will never cease to be taunted, when occasion may require it, that they are below par as to caste on their mother's side. But where large numbers of the community are similarly situated, there is not much room for reproach.

We now give a case of recent occurrence on the other side. A man of wealth and education, and high in office, in another part of the island, but of low caste, has purchased with a great sum the privilege of marrying the daughter of one of our schoolmasters of the Vellala caste, of the highest grade. By this the native gentleman is brought into alliance with the whole family circle of a superior caste; and this will in various ways be made to operate favorably upon his posterity. From these two cases, which are illustrative of what is extensively in progress in the country, it will be seen that caste, whatever it may be, is an article in the market, which may be turned into silver and gold, and consequently is of substantial value.

Under this aspect, caste may be regarded as an order of nobility, which may be shared by those who are in circumstances to make the purchase. Under such influences, however, caste must vary in its nature, and ultimately exhaust itself by expansion.

But alas for the nobility of caste! Causes are now in operation, in this Province, which tend to destroy the foundation on which caste, as a civil distinction, has hitherto rested its claims. In former times, under the native kings and princes, the Vellalas and Madapalies were privileged orders in the community; and the results of those privileges have operated favorably upon their posterity from generation to generation. But now, times have so altered, that "on the scale of wealth, talents, industry, and moral character," caste, whether in the Hindoo sense of it, or as a civil distinction, can confer but little elevation, nor the absence of it impose but little degradation. This will more clearly appear as we proceed,

3. To show what the English government has done, both directly and indirectly, for the destruction of caste.

(1.) By the abolition of Slavery, which took place soon after our settlement in the island. By that important measure several castes, such as Covias, Pollas, Malavas and others, were placed on a new footing in society, and are gradually rising towards an equality with their former masters in wealth, intelligence and importance.

(2.) By disregarding, to a great extent, the claims of caste, and placing applicants for office on the high ground of personal qualification, trustworthiness, efficiency in business, etc., the government has wrought extensively and powerfully for good upon the whole native population, but most subversively to the claims of caste.

(3.) By an effectual injunction upon European magistrates and native head-men not to enter the caste of individuals in public documents, such as suits at law, deeds, registries, jury-lists, etc., government is doing much to obliterate even the remembrance of caste distinctions from the public mind.

(4.) By encouraging the sale of arrack and toddy, the government is doing much to destroy caste distinctions. Drunkenness is a great leveler. Even some of the brahmins and Vellalas are becoming familiar with the use of intoxicating drinks, while some of the lower castes do not drink. Thus, while the low-castes are rising, some of the high-castes are falling by intemperance.

We will now present a few miscellaneous remarks on the peculiarities of caste in our mission field.

1. The three higher castes, (leaving out the brahmins,) viz., the Vellalas, Madapalies and Chitties, form a large majority of the population of the Province. Of these three castes, the Vellalas are far more numerous than the other two. As society was constructed under the rule of the native princes, the Vellalas were the agriculturists of the country, and in this Province the owners of the soil. As the lords of the country, they held most of the other castes in their service, by different tenures, and on different terms of service,—a bond of union well understood by the parties, pervading the whole community, and binding them together by different interests. The two great divisions of these *under* classes were, *first*, The three castes of slaves that have been already mentioned; and *secondly*, The Kudimakkal, that is, the blacksmiths, carpenters, barbers, washermen and goldsmiths of the country, including the Pariahs, who are tom-tom beaters, and drudges in various employments.

From the very beginning, we have opened our great commission to the whole population of the country, as far as our circumstances would allow; but it is a remarkable fact, which we cannot satisfactorily account for, and which is one of the most characteristic features of our mission field, that the three higher castes, more especially the Vellalas, are almost exclusively the people who have opened unto us, and thus secured the advantages of our mission labors. The Kudimakkals were from the beginning among our most constant hearers, daily, while employed in our service in week times, and weekly at church on the Sabbath; but almost without exception, all this numerous class have rejected the Gospel, and but few of them have ever manifested an interest in sending their children to our common schools.

From these remarks we must except those of the Fisher caste, who are a people more independent of the Vellalas, and from whom a portion of our converts have been gathered. But the Vellalas are emphatically our people; and notwithstanding the losses they have sustained by the freedom of their slaves, and by the introduction of the principles of liberty and equality in society, yet combining the advantages of Christian instruction and of a superior education with the advantages which they inherited from their fathers, they will long continue to be the most thriving, energetic, intelligent and best behaved portion of the Tamil population. On this account it will continue to be a desideratum to belong to the Vellala caste.

2. Another feature of our mission field bearing on the subject in hand, is, that in most of the numerous and populous villages into which the whole Province is divided, the different castes are found in due proportion, while those of the same caste in the villages round are more or less related to each other. On this account, and on account of the dense population of the whole Province, it will be physically impossible, even were it thought desirable, for us to separate them into Christian villages, as in Tinnevelly, and in some other parts of the Continent.

We have made arrangements so to proceed in our work of discipling the whole mass of the population, that every one may continue in the place wherein he was called with the least disturbance possible. This we consider as the dictate of wisdom and prudence, till they be made to understand what be the first principles of the oracles of God, the sum and substance of which is love to God and love to man. If, indeed, we could have whole villages of the same caste, we might prosecute our evangelical labors without rousing and stimulating some of the worst principles and passions of our fallen nature. But as it is, we think it not wise to disturb the present arrangements of society, except by the silent operations of the Gospel of Christ. We would make the most of the injunction, "Go home to thy friends, and tell how great things the Lord hath done for thee, and hath had compassion on thee." And thus would we cause the people to understand, that excision from the family circle is not a necessary adjunct of one's becoming a Christian, but rather that he thereby becomes a better son, or brother, husband, or father, than before his conversion. We consider it safer, and a more satisfactory trial of one's sincerity, to live as a Christian among his friends, than to be separated from them in a Christian village.

3. We formerly thought the evils of caste arose chiefly from the unreasonable exactions and pressures of the higher upon the lower castes; and this was doubtless the case in former times. But one of the results of our observation while dealing with caste, as things now are, is that the spirit of the low caste rising, is as much to be deprecated as the spirit of the high caste reigning. "For three things the earth is disquieted; yea, for four things which it cannot bear." One of the four is, "for a servant when he reigneth." Proverbs xxx. 21. This point admits of extensive illustration from scenes and occurrences too familiar to our minds to invite a recital, and moreover it is too obvious to require formal proof. We will therefore remark generally, as the result of our experience, that since we have found by our adventures that the enemy with which we have to contend cannot be slain by carnal weapons, we are very slow to pitch battle, or to come into direct and hostile collision with caste, as we now find it in this Province. We are fully convinced

there is a far "more excellent way" of dealing with it. More especially has this been the case since we have better understood the structure of Hindoo society, and learned to what extent the different castes in this Province answer to the different classes of nobility, gentry, merchants, mechanics, farmers, and menial servants in Protestant Christendom.

The principal canon we would lay down on this subject is, to tolerate nothing within our control, which militates against our ruling the house of God, or watching over, guiding and disciplining the church of Christ, according to the law and directory which he himself has given us. "For now we live, if our churches stand fast in the Lord." If asked whether we do not allow persons to remain in our churches, who entertain erroneous views, or who give place to unhallowed feelings on the subject of caste, our reply is, that we do; but in the sense only in which we make recognition of the fact, that in all cases of regeneration the "old man" is destined to coexist simultaneously with the new, until by a successful exercise of the ministry "for the perfecting of the saints," they "all come to the unity of the faith, into the measure of the stature of the fullness of Christ." "We have learned, by our experience and observation, that caste is a great evil; an evil which governs the religious emotions, tastes and habits of all the races of India; which is imbibed by the infant at the breast, and cherished with scrupulous anxiety through life; an evil which has been ingrained into the whole Hindoo character, for well nigh three thousand years, so as to form the very cement of Hindooism." What then? By the preaching of the word to a man full-grown under the regimen above described, a ray of light and a principle of life have been imparted from Him who is "the light" and "the life of men." The giant caste-man has become, as we fondly hope, a man of God; but to such an extent a weakling that he is like unto a "bruised reed and smoking flax." We submit the question, as to what are the appropriate instrumentalities by which we may in the first place unmake, and then reform this man of giant growth? Are there any appropriate appliances for this purpose but the Gospel ministry, the training and discipline of the Christian church, and the concurring influences of God, the Holy Ghost? The Bishop of Calcutta remarks: "In this diocese the first thing a catechumen does, is, to reject caste *in toto*." What can this remark mean, in view of the foregoing description of the "giant evil?" Every Hindoo, when he enters the Christian church by baptism, when he eats from the same plate and drinks from the same cup with those of an inferior grade, does to a certain extent renounce caste. He ought to do it "*in toto*." But his caste feelings and prejudices are not thereby wholly eradicated, and cannot be in a moment. It is a work of time. The appropriate means for abolishing caste, in every desirable sense of the expression, are, we believe, light and love on the part of the missionaries, docility and growth in piety on the part of the native converts, together with the promised influences of the Holy Spirit. All compulsory means used for this purpose, in which we cannot carry with us the judgment and consciences of those concerned, are generally disastrous to the assailants and the assailed—to the Christian church, and to the heathen population at large.

We trust the foregoing pages will be sufficient to meet your first request, that we furnish "some positive statements on the general subject of caste."

But you ask definitely, "How do you treat caste in your churches, and among your church members in the walks of private and social life?" We have never allowed caste in our churches. We have never allowed any separate communion for high and low castes, as was formerly the custom in Southern India. All our members, both high and low caste, have, from the beginning, drunk wine from the same cup, and eaten bread from the same plate, and this promiscuously.

But you inquire as to how we treat caste "in the walks of private and social life?" This awakens our attention to the necessity of briefly showing to what extent there is and must be a non-interference between the missionaries and the families of their converts. In endeavoring to give you some further idea on this subject, we remark, that a Hindoo—find him where you will—may justly be defined to be an embodiment of rites and observances peculiar to the Hindoo race. These observances, customs and manners, may be divided into three classes.

1. Nationalities, or that which is common to all castes and classes.

2. Idolatrous observances.

3. Caste distinctions and usages.

Of these three classes the first has the greatest, and the last, perhaps, the least prominence in the general characteristics of the nation, and more especially so in relation to the point under consideration; that is, in the walks of private and social life. We do not, in our social intercourse with them, readily recognize the respective castes beyond our own personal acquaintance, and beyond what may be known by the fact that several of the lower castes are, from their very positions in society, low, untidy and repulsive. On this ground, whatever may have been the cause of their degradation, there is as substantial a distinction of castes or classes, which cannot but be observed, as between the sons of noblemen and the children of the "ragged schools" of England. A distinct recognition of this fact, is of fundamental importance in all attempts to bring or to push the extremes of society to associate, and especially to eat together, in private houses.

We will now give a few specimens of nationalities, studiously avoiding all that appertains either to caste distinctions or idolatrous observances.

1. The Hindoos have no *home*, in our sense of the word; no place where the family come familiarly together, in a social way, where they may be seen. When we visit a family, we do not enter the house, but tarry without, either in the yard or the verandah, and speak with those who make their appearance. This we do, either standing, or seated on an inverted rice mortar, or in some other position. All are interested to know the specific object, for which the missionary has come to the premises; but their sense of propriety and good manners do not require the family to assemble. Even Christian families are slow to make their appearance, although called. As Hindoos, they ought not to appear at all, but continue in the house and at their work. Those Christian families in which both husband and wife have been educated in our boarding schools, are far in advance of their countrymen. Still they are but Hindoos in a state of gradual transition, and living, it may be, in the houses of their parents.

2. For very good reasons, we do not encourage, even in our boarding schools, any important changes of the native customs of the Hindoos, in regard to dress, manner of living, mode of sitting, furnishing their houses, etc. In all these particulars there are some improvements, but no imitation of European manners and customs. Such an imitation would be adverse to the great object we have in view, of operating upon the mass of the population through the agency of the educated classes. If even the educated should adopt the European dress, and other concomitant customs, they would lose credit in the estimation of their countrymen, and be subjected to fourfold greater expenses, with less of real comfort and independence of life and character.

3. The uneducated Hindoo does not ordinarily make use of chairs, tables, bedsteads, etc., seeing that the whole ground floor of the house, with appropriate matting, is available for all these purposes. And what, in their view, is the use of crockery, knives and forks, and spoons, and the whole profusion of table furniture, seeing that a few articles of earthen ware for cooking rice and curry, a brass pot for water, and a garden with plantain leaves for plates, with his own right hand for a spoon, are a full supply in this line of service? The act of eating is a rite and ceremony to be performed in private. Even men are not willing to be seen eating by any one who does not join them in the act. But for a woman to allow herself to be seen eating, would be a positive disgrace. In this vulgar exercise the right hand is so deeply involved, and so important is it that the business be finished at a sitting, that the most menial servant has a substantial reason for turning a deaf ear to his master's call, or thinks it sufficient if his master knows that he is eating. How then can the wife possibly eat with her husband and children, and male guests, while she is mistress of the ceremonies? European wives may do this, as they have domestics to wait upon the table. Custom has made it the duty of the wife to deal out the rice and curry, and to bring water for drinking and washing after the meal is finished. But while the Hindoo woman may not be seen eating common food, she may be seen enjoying the betel leaf and areca nut as an honorary repast.

It is a nationality, also, that sons who are beyond early childhood, do not converse freely with their father, nor even with others in their father's presence. Nor should an elder and a younger brother sit in public on the same mat or seat, nor should a son-in-law speak with his mother-in-law, nor a father-in-law be present with his daughter-in-law, etc., etc. These are mere specimens of nationalities, common to all castes; and most of them are most rigidly observed by those who would be accounted the higher grades of society.

Again, when we are visited by the natives, it is generally either in the way of business, or of attendance at religious meetings, or of private instructions; and then, with a few exceptions, they are seated on a mat, as is customary with them at their own houses, and in the church of God. Occasionally our native preachers and a few others sit on chairs at our tables, and partake with us of a cup of tea, fruit, bread, etc.

Many other instances might be given of customs, which are mere nationalities, and which have no particular connection with caste. Indeed we find a practical difficulty in attempting to separate purely caste distinctions, in the customs of social life, from mere nationalities; and it is even more difficult in the mind of a native. Even Christians are prone to plead for customs, which we believe are contrary to the spirit of the Gospel, that they are mere nationalities; while the unconverted Hindoo sees no more propriety in our requiring a convert to break or renounce his caste, than to break or renounce other nationalities.

By the specimens of nationalities, which we have given above, it will be readily understood that it cannot be expected that we, as foreigners, whose customs and manners we would not have them imitate, should act the part of reformers of the Hindoos "in the walks of private and social life," except so far as these customs are contrary to the spirit of the Gospel. But while we thus speak of the great gulf of nationalities, which separate us from the people, we rejoice to be able to say, that we have a growing esteem for and an increasing attachment to the Hindoo nation as our people, and as a people to be made ready for the Lord. Many of them will, we doubt not, be a crown of rejoicing in the day of the Lord Jesus, to those who labor with fidelity and perseverance for their conversion. Even now, and with blest anticipations, we come into close contact with them, holding constant and delightful intercourse with both the rising and the risen generation, on all subjects appertaining to the great object of our residence among them.

But you ask, "How far are the Continental castes, and the castes on the Island, alike? And why do you not treat caste as they do on the Continent?"

In answer to the first question, we must commence by saying, that with one exception, we have none of us, for any length of time, resided on the Continent, and are therefore quite unable to do justice to this subject. Our local and intimate knowledge of caste, as it exists there, is not sufficient to enable us to make that definite and exact comparison which you wish. You will perceive, however, that we have in fact said many things in the former part of this letter which are an appropriate answer to your question. By the quotation which we made from the Madras Document, you will see a very carefully worded definition of caste, as it is supposed to exist on the Continent. And by comparing this with the statements we have made as to caste, as we find it in this Province, you will clearly perceive, that it has already, by various causes, been greatly modified; and especially that there are now many causes in operation tending powerfully and rapidly to do away with the evil.

But, "Why do you not treat caste as they do on the Continent?"

We have already stated facts to show that our circumstances, with respect to this evil, differ widely from those of missionaries laboring on the Continent.

But we will say:

1. That we believe it is not proper for us to legislate upon this subject for the members of our churches, to compel the high castes to do violence to all their views

of propriety, by eating in the houses of those of low caste, or to intermarry with them. But we have, from the commencement of our mission to the present time, used all Scriptural arguments against the distinctions of caste, and we think with great effect. It is hardly necessary for us to repeat, that we have never allowed any distinctions of caste in our churches. Different castes have also been in the habit of eating together in our boarding schools. Many of our native assistants, in certain circumstances, will cheerfully eat with those of lower castes, especially when on tours. At our Annual Convocation, in September, at Batticotta, provision is made for all our church members, and very many of different castes eat together on that occasion ; not by compulsion, but willingly. Our native assistants, also, most cheerfully go among the low castes, preach the Gospel, and superintend schools. They also assist them in sickness, and at funerals. But to make a law, compelling the high castes to eat in the houses of low castes, or to intermarry with them, would be more abhorrent to their feelings and all their views of propriety, than for a law to be passed for the churches in New York or Boston compelling the rich to receive their servants, both black and white, to their tables. We do not believe that it is proper for us to legislate upon this subject.

2. We should not accomplish the object we have in view.

Our object is to destroy caste, and especially to root it out of the minds of our native converts.

Now it is a well known fact, that many native assistants and schoolmasters, rather than lose their employment, and be thrown into great pecuniary embarrassment, will comply, for the time being, with the demands of the missionaries to eat food prepared by low castes ; and they justify themselves in this matter, and their friends also excuse them and overlook it, simply because they are compelled to do it, or sacrifice their living. But is the caste principle thus extinguished, or even diminished in their breasts? We think not. We do not believe that leviathan is thus tamed.

3. This course is productive of positive evils.

It sours their minds; and its tendency is to make our members act hypocritically in this matter. Unless we can enlighten their minds, and carry their consciences with us, we gain nothing but their displeasure. We do not accomplish our object. For the caste feeling in their minds is rather strengthened, than diminished, by this course. We will encourage them, and help them in every possible way to do away with the evils of caste; and we fully believe that the only proper way of accomplishing this object is by light and love, and example, and the power of the Spirit of God. By the diligent use of these means, in connection with what the government is doing on this subject, we believe that caste is rapidly losing ground in this province. How long it will linger, we cannot say. But this we do know, by long experience, that it cannot be killed by violence.

We see clearly, that it is the natural tendency of the Gospel to elevate the low castes to a level with the high, rather than to bring down the high castes to a level with the low; and this it will in due time accomplish. It will certainly, also, teach the high castes to treat their brethren below them with Christian kindness and love.

In behalf of the mission:

Benjamin C. Meigs,
Daniel Poor,
William W. Howland.

www.ingramcontent.com/pod-product-compliance
Lightning Source LLC
LaVergne TN
LVHW011138110826
845150LV00008B/2388
9781418193386